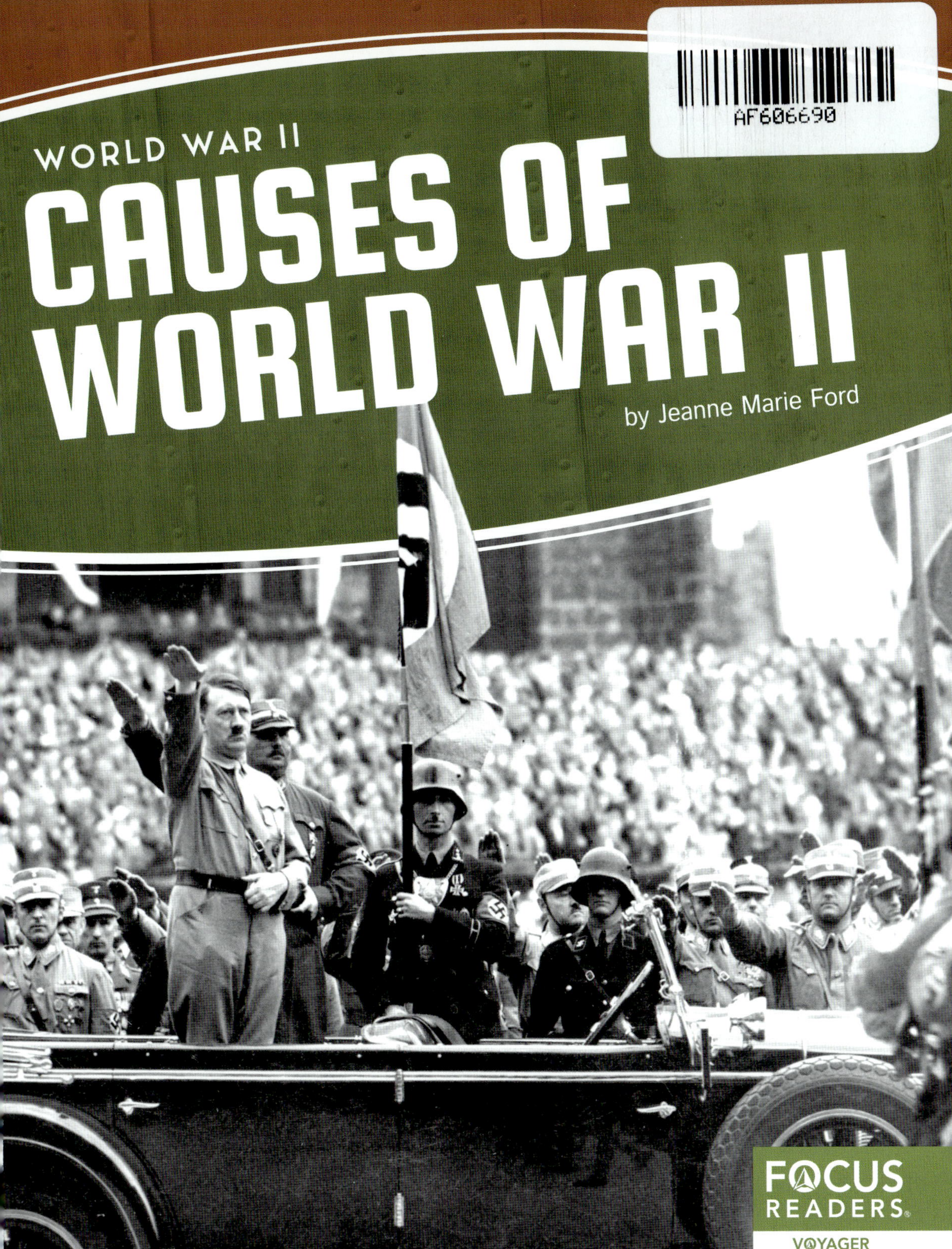

WORLD WAR II

CAUSES OF WORLD WAR II

by Jeanne Marie Ford

FOCUS READERS
VOYAGER

www.focusreaders.com

Focus Readers is distributed by North Star Editions:
sales@northstareditions.com | 888-417-0195

Produced for Focus Readers by Red Line Editorial.

Content Consultant: Dr. Gideon Mailer, Associate Professor of History, University of Minnesota Duluth

Photographs ©: Berliner Verlag/Archiv/Picture Alliance/DPA/AP Images, cover, 1; Shutterstock Images, 4–5, 7 (left), 7 (right), 8, 10–11, 15, 21, 24, 26, 28–29, 31, 33, 35, 36–37, 39, 41, 42–43, 45; AP Images, 13, 18–19, 22–23; Photo 12/Archives Snark/Alamy, 17

Library of Congress Cataloging-in-Publication Data
Names: Ford, Jeanne Marie, 1971- author.
Title: Causes of World War II / by Jeanne Marie Ford.
Description: Lake Elmo, MN : Focus Readers, [2023] | Series: World War II | Includes index. | Audience: Grades 4-6
Identifiers: LCCN 2022007149 (print) | LCCN 2022007150 (ebook) | ISBN 9781637392812 (hardcover) | ISBN 9781637393338 (paperback) | ISBN 9781637394311 (pdf) | ISBN 9781637393857 (ebook)
Subjects: LCSH: World War, 1939-1945--Causes--Juvenile literature.
Classification: LCC D741 .F66 2023 (print) | LCC D741 (ebook) | DDC 940.53--dc23/eng/20220217
LC record available at https://lccn.loc.gov/2022007149
LC ebook record available at https://lccn.loc.gov/2022007150

Printed in the United States of America
Mankato, MN
082022

ABOUT THE AUTHOR

Jeanne Marie Ford is an Emmy-winning TV scriptwriter and holds an MFA in writing for children from Vermont College. She has written numerous children's books and articles and also teaches college English. She lives in Maryland with her husband and two children.

TABLE OF CONTENTS

THIS IS "DER TAG

DETROIT, MICHIGAN.

GERMANY WAKES OUT OF DREAM OF EMPIRE

NEW YORK.

GREATEST WAR IN HISTORY OF THE

PEACE

CINCIN

GERMANS AFFIX SIG TO COMPACT IN P OF ENVOYS FROM

WASHINGTON, D. C., SATURDAY, JU

IGN TREATY

New York, Sonntag, den 29. Juni 1919.

Friede

Der Weltkrieg

PRESIDENT WILSON'S CABLED MESSAGE TO THE AMERICAN PEOPLE:

"The treaty of peace has been signed. If it is ratified and acted upon in full and sincere execution of its terms it will furnish the charter for a new order of affairs in the world. It is a severe treaty in the duties and penalties it imposes upon Germany, but it is severe only because great wrongs done by Germany are to be righted and repaired; it imposes nothing that Germany cannot do; and she can regain her rightful standing in the world by the prompt and honorable fulfillment of its terms. And it is much more than a treaty of peace with Germany. * * * It makes international law a reality supported by imperative sanction. * * * It recognizes the inalienable rights of nationality, the rights of minorities and the sanctity of religious belief and practice. * * * It is for this reason that I have spoken of it as a great charter for a new order of affairs. There is ground here for deep satisfaction, universal re-assurance, and confident hope."

WAR FORMA

ED WHEN 26 N

PPROVE THE

New-Yorker Staats-Zeitung, 29.

Friedensfch

PREMIER CLEMENCEAU TO FRENCH DEPUTIES:

"By France and by our allies the work of the salvation of the world from peril is accomplished, on the single condition that we remain at our posts of duty. The old spirit of warlike domination is perhaps mastered forever. The day has come when force and justice, that were redoubtedly separated, must be rejoined for the peace of peoples that humanity may live. That peace we want with a will that nothing should shake. We will make that peace, as we made war, without weakness."

Friedens-

, Bringing War to an E

arks Formalities at Versa

in Message Urges Acceptance

EATY SIGNED BY

KING GEORGE'S A THE BRITISH PEOP

"The signing of the trea be received with deep throughout the British formal act brings to stages the terrible war w astated Europe. It m victory of ideals, of free liberty for which we have sacrifices. I share my peop thanksgiving and earnestly the coming years of peace m them ever-increasing happ prosperity."

SUNDAY MORNING

CONQUERED GERMANS SIGN

RICHMOND, VA.

GERMAN DREAM OF W CONTROL ENDS AS AGENTS SIGN PEA

World War

No. 12,471—P. M.

XTRA

TREATY

Times

CHAPTER 1

AN UNEASY PEACE

World War I raged from 1914 to 1918. More than 30 countries were involved. Approximately 20 million people died. Survivors wanted to make sure such a huge war would never happen again.

With this goal in mind, representatives from several nations met in France in 1919. A group of countries known as the Allies had won the war. They agreed to make peace with Germany, which

World War I was often called "The War to End All Wars." People hoped peace would follow it.

had fought on the losing side. The Allies wanted to keep Germany from attacking again. So, the peace **treaty** required Germany to give up land and weapons. Germany had to admit guilt for causing the war. And it had to pay **reparations** to the Allies.

Germany signed the Treaty of Versailles on June 19. Many Germans were surprised and angered by their country's defeat. They felt the treaty was unfair. And they blamed Germany's government for many of the country's problems.

Germany was not the only country upset by the treaty. Before World War I, Germany had held territories in China. But the Treaty of Versailles gave these territories to Japan. Japan and China had both joined the Allies in World War I. Before that, however, the two nations had been enemies. After the war, tensions rose between them again.

Many Chinese people felt the treaty unfairly favored Japan.

In 1920, the Allies formed a group called the League of Nations. It aimed to keep peace around the world. However, some major nations decided not to join. They included the United States, Germany, and the Soviet Union. As a result, the League of Nations didn't have much power.

EUROPE BEFORE AND AFTER WWI

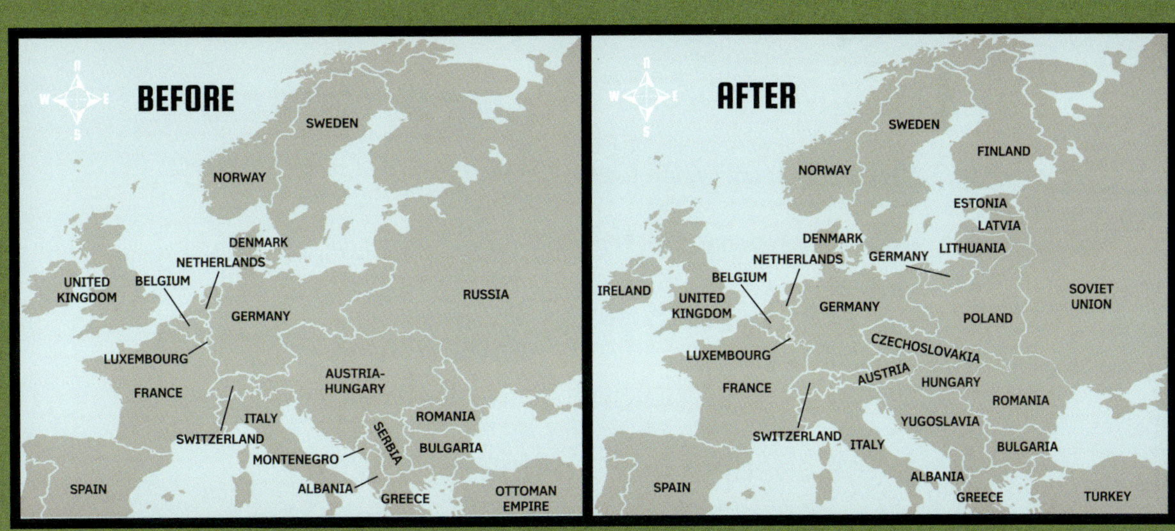

During World War I, armies fought in trenches. Land near these trenches was often completely destroyed.

During this time, many countries faced crippling poverty. World War I had damaged huge areas of land. Many of Europe's towns, farms, and factories had been destroyed. As a result, millions of people struggled to get food or work.

Many countries couldn't collect enough taxes to cover the costs of war. To pay their bills, they printed more money. Money decreased in value as a result. Losing nations also had to pay reparations. So, they printed even more money. This led to a problem called **hyperinflation**.

In 1922, Germany missed a reparations payment. French and Belgian soldiers marched into Germany in response. They planned to seize goods and factories. The German government told the factory workers to **strike**. It also printed more money to pay them. This money sent the country's inflation out of control. Prices rose so fast people needed wheelbarrows of money to buy everyday items such as bread. Some people burned money for fuel because it cost less than wood.

In 1929, a new crisis struck. The US stock market crashed, and a global **depression** followed. Millions of people around the world became very poor. Many became desperate, too. These problems led to even more unrest.

CHAPTER 2

THE RISE OF HITLER

World War I left many people feeling uneasy about the future. Some people began turning to politicians with extreme views. One of these extreme leaders was Adolf Hitler. Hitler was angry about the way World War I had ended. He hated the terms the Allies had forced on Germany. And he blamed Germany's government, the Weimar Republic, for accepting those terms.

Adolf Hitler led the Nazis, a racist and nationalist group that rose to power in Germany.

In 1919, Hitler joined a political party that opposed the Weimar Republic. The group soon became known as the Nazi Party. By mid-1921, Hitler was the party's leader.

The Nazi Party was based on fascist ideas. Fascists believe countries should have one strong leader. They often believe one nation is better than all others. And they tend to use violence to support their views.

For example, Benito Mussolini led the National Fascist Party in Italy. Mussolini organized his followers into groups of fighters known as Blackshirts. They attacked people who disagreed with Mussolini. Hitler admired Mussolini. He formed his own army, called the Storm Troopers. They attacked enemies of the Nazis.

Hitler knew Germans were eager to blame someone for their country's defeat. So, he gave

Benito Mussolini (center, arm raised) became Italy's leader in 1922. By 1925, he had named himself dictator.

hateful speeches against Jews. Hitler accused Jews of causing Germany's problems. He said they ruined the greatness of "true" Germans. By spreading these racist ideas, Nazis gained political power.

In 1923, Hitler led a rebellion against the Weimar Republic. It failed, and police arrested him. The government banned the Nazi Party in Germany. Hitler was sentenced to prison.

However, he was released after a few months. In 1925, Hitler promised to seek power only through elections. He also convinced German leaders to lift the ban on the Nazi Party.

Germany's economy suffered during the early 1930s. Many citizens felt desperate. They wanted change. The Nazis' promises of greatness appealed to them. By 1932, Nazis had more seats in Germany's **parliament** than any other party. They also had 400,000 Storm Troopers.

In January 1933, the German president made Hitler the country's chancellor, or parliamentary leader. The president believed he could control Hitler. He planned to use the Nazis' popularity to increase his own power. However, this idea backfired.

In February 1933, a fire broke out in the parliament building. Hitler used the panic

Hitler held parades and rallies to build support for the Nazi Party.

after the fire to gain even more power. Nazi leaders persuaded Germany's president to pass emergency laws. They claimed the laws would prevent more unrest. But the laws limited people's freedoms.

In 1934, the German president died. Hitler named himself the supreme ruler of the German people. He made German soldiers declare an oath of loyalty to him. The Nazis now controlled every part of life in Germany.

PROPAGANDA

Both Hitler and Mussolini used propaganda to spread their views. Propaganda is information that manipulates people's beliefs and behavior. It is designed to be persuasive. In many cases, it is also untrue.

Before his rise to power, Mussolini had worked as a journalist. He knew how easily the press could change people's minds. So, he made sure it supported his views. He forced journalists to say only good things about him. And he banned his political opponents. By controlling what people could read, Mussolini shaped what they thought.

Hitler used propaganda to help the Nazis gain and keep power. Nazi propaganda came in many forms. It spread messages through art, newspapers, and radio. Some told Germans to blame Jews for their troubles. Others described violent acts against Jews as keeping peace. These

Nazi propaganda urged Germans to support their country's leaders and war effort.

claims were not true. But when people heard these lies often enough, they began to believe them.

Nazi propaganda also tried to inspire loyalty for Hitler and Germany. Nazis wanted Germans to believe their country was better than all others. And they wanted Germans to support invading other areas. At the same time, Nazis used propaganda to mislead other countries about Hitler's intentions. They said he wanted only a few small changes. They hid his true goals.

CHAPTER 3

THE SPANISH CIVIL WAR

In 1936, Spain plunged into civil war. Spain's government was led by **socialists**. However, the Spanish military tried to take over. It was led by Francisco Franco, who had ties to fascists.

Other countries soon got involved. The Soviet Union supported Spain's socialist government. Meanwhile, Germany and Italy supported Franco. People from around the world flooded into Spain to join the fight. Most sided against Franco.

Francisco Franco rose to power during Spain's civil war. He ruled until his death in 1975.

During the Spanish Civil War, soldiers began using many new weapons and **tactics**. Airplanes had played a limited role in previous wars. But Germany had developed a strong new air force. These German planes dropped bombs on battlefields. They also bombed hospitals, schools, and churches. In past wars, fighting had focused on enemy armies. **Civilians** hadn't usually been attacked. Now, the Germans were deliberately targeting them. They hoped to make people afraid. They wanted them to give up.

In 1936, Madrid was the first European capital to be bombed from the air. In 1937, German bombs destroyed the town of Guernica. Italian planes bombed other parts of Spain. Fear spread throughout the country.

Both sides used torture and violence. Many civilians were brutally attacked. Half a million

Many civilians lost their homes during the attacks on Madrid.

Spaniards were imprisoned in concentration camps. They were forced to work or to fight for Franco. Many were sent to military trials and killed.

In 1939, Franco's side won the war. Experts estimate that 500,000 people had died. Plus, hundreds of thousands had fled the country. Military planners took note. Extending war beyond the battlefield had proved to be an effective strategy.

CHAPTER 4

JAPAN ON THE MARCH

Meanwhile, trouble was brewing in Asia. Japan had fought on the side of the Allies during World War I. It wanted to be seen as a growing world power. However, Japan felt the Treaty of Versailles unfairly favored Western countries.

After World War I, Japan worked to expand its power. It looked to the Chinese region of Manchuria. This area had large amounts of land and raw materials. These resources could help

Throughout the 1930s, thousands of Japanese soldiers poured into Manchuria, a region of China.

supply Japan's growing population. So, Japan invaded Manchuria in 1931. Many Japanese people moved to the area.

China protested Japan's action to the League of Nations. The league issued a report. It said Manchuria should be returned to China. And it ordered Japan to remove its troops. Japan ignored

JAPANESE INVASION OF CHINA

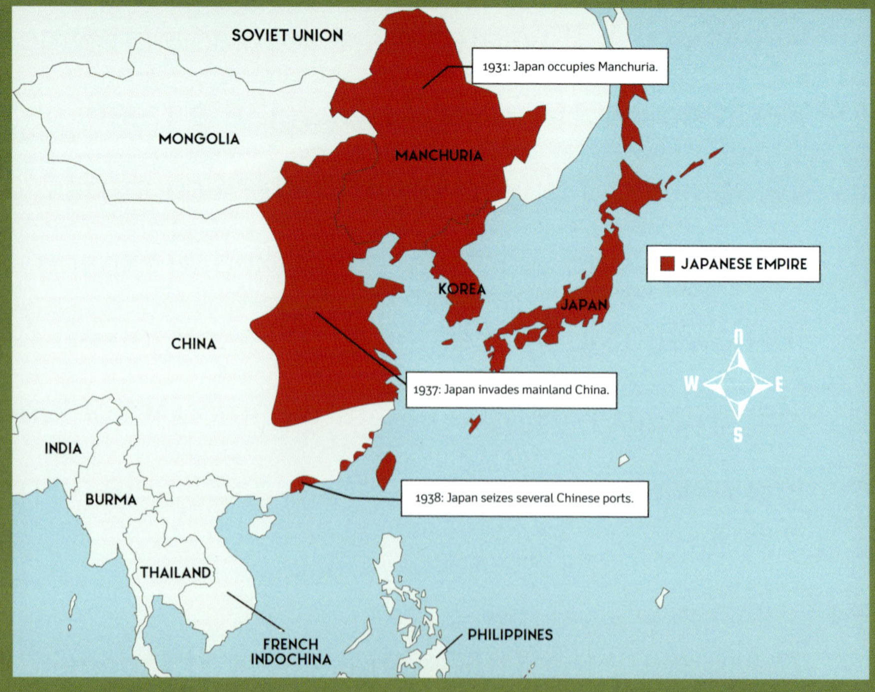

this order. The league didn't force Japanese troops to leave. Still, Japanese leaders were angry that the league had sided with China. So, in 1933, Japan left the League of Nations.

Throughout the 1930s, Japan continued to expand its power. The military and police took control of much of the government. Leaders controlled the information sent out by the media. They also shaped what people learned in schools. Students were taught to worship the emperor. They were also told Japan was favored by God. Like some Germans, some Japanese people believed their nation was the best.

CONSIDER THIS

How does controlling what people learn in schools affect a government's power?

As they invaded China, Japanese soldiers often treated its people with great cruelty.

The Japanese army grew more and more powerful. In February 1936, soldiers killed top officials and tried to take over the government. Their attempt failed. But the military's influence continued to grow.

Hitler was keeping a close eye on Japan's increasing power. He predicted that Japan would soon clash with the Soviet Union. The two countries had been enemies in the past. Hitler thought Japan would easily defeat the Soviets. So, he decided to make an alliance with Japan. Hitler believed this alliance would help both countries. By becoming partners, Germany and Japan could fight the Soviet Union together.

Japan's leaders agreed. In November 1936, Germany and Japan signed the Anti-Comintern Pact. They agreed to oppose the spread of **Communism** and Communist countries. Italy joined the agreement a year later.

On July 7, 1937, Japan launched another invasion into China. This attack brought territory beyond Manchuria under Japanese control. Japanese soldiers poured into China. The brutal invasion lasted for years. During that time, Japan took over land in northeast China. Japanese soldiers bombed cities. Thousands of Chinese soldiers and civilians were killed. The world was marching toward another war.

CHAPTER 5

GERMAN EXPANSION

After Japan took over Manchuria, other nations made land grabs. In 1935, Italy invaded Ethiopia. Once again, the League of Nations made a weak response.

European leaders watched Hitler nervously. They knew he wanted to gain land and resources for Germany. Hitler wanted all people of German ancestry to be part of one large country. He hoped to expand Germany's borders into Eastern Europe.

Throughout the 1930s, Germany built up its army and air force.

During the 1930s, Germany had ignored the Treaty of Versailles and begun rebuilding its army. Many leaders worried that Hitler was planning an attack. However, none of the former Allies wanted another war. So, they tried very hard to keep the peace.

The French built the Maginot Line. It was a set of defenses that ran along their border with Germany. The French believed these defenses would keep them safe from German attacks. The British and French also made a plan for dealing with Hitler. They decided to use **appeasement**. They hoped that if they gave in to Hitler's demands, he would soon be satisfied. Meanwhile, the United States tried to stay out of foreign conflicts completely.

In 1936, Hitler sent troops into a part of western Germany called the Rhineland. According

The Maginot Line was a series of guns and barricades designed to block a German attack on France.

to the Treaty of Versailles, this action was not allowed. However, France didn't want to fight without Britain's support. And Britain thought it was France's problem. Therefore, no one did anything to stop Hitler.

Hitler was also gathering allies. Germany and Italy had been enemies in World War I. But they both supported Franco in the Spanish Civil War. Mussolini and Hitler also shared similar ideas. In October 1936, they signed an agreement. They formed the Rome-Berlin Axis. They hoped to become the most powerful nations in Europe.

Hitler felt confident that Germany could take over nearby countries and get away with it. His next target was Austria. Austria was a German-speaking country. Hitler wanted to join it with Germany. German soldiers marched into Austria on March 12, 1938. A day later, the two countries were united. Most Austrians supported this action.

Next, Hitler set his sights on a part of Czechoslovakia called the Sudetenland. Many Germans lived in this area. It also held many natural resources. In 1938, Hitler threatened war

CONSIDER THIS

Do you think appeasement is ever a good idea? Why or why not?

Germany's takeover of Austria was known as the Anschluss.

if the Allies tried to stop him from taking it. So, Britain, Italy, Germany, and France signed the Munich Agreement. They agreed not to interfere if Hitler promised not to invade anywhere else.

Britain's prime minister, Neville Chamberlain, believed appeasement was working. He thought Hitler would keep the agreement. Other leaders were growing uneasy. Every time they gave Hitler what he wanted, he seemed to demand more.

ANTI-SEMITISM

As Hitler's power spread, so did his attacks on Jews. Germany passed laws that made life difficult for Jewish people. Some laws said Jews couldn't hold certain jobs or attend school. Others limited where Jews could live, shop, or travel.

In 1933, the Nazis began using concentration camps. At first, the camps held political prisoners. But Nazis later sent Jews and anyone else they disliked there, too. Conditions in the camps were terrible. By 1938, thousands of people had died.

On November 7, 1938, a Jewish student shot and killed a German official. The student wanted to protest how his family had been mistreated. But Nazis used the event as an excuse to target Jews. On November 9, Nazis destroyed thousands of Jewish businesses and places of worship in Germany and Austria. More than 90 Jewish people

Nazis put up signs telling Germans not to shop at stores owned by Jewish people.

were killed. The event was known as Kristallnacht, or the Night of Broken Glass.

The next morning, thousands of Jewish men were arrested. Most were sent to concentration camps. Other countries condemned the Nazis' actions. But they feared war with Germany. So, most did little else to help the Jews.

Modewaren

CHAPTER 6

WAR IN EUROPE

The Sudetenland held most of Czechoslovakia's coal, electricity, steel, and iron. Now these resources belonged to Hitler. Czech leaders feared Hitler would try to grab even more land. They tried to appease him. But once again, this strategy failed.

In March 1939, Hitler invaded the rest of Czechoslovakia. Within a day, two provinces had

Some parts of Eastern Europe deeply opposed the Nazis. Others supported Hitler.

fallen to Germany. Hungary moved in and claimed the southern part of the country.

By invading Czechoslovakia, Hitler broke the Munich Agreement. But once again, the League of Nations did nothing. Instead of facing consequences, Hitler was stronger than ever. Germany had gained control of Czech weapons and airfields. Plus, Hitler had taken land where non-Germans lived. His plans clearly went beyond taking back German territory.

Hitler continued to look for ways to increase his power. In May 1939, he and Mussolini signed the Pact of Steel. This pact was a stronger version of the Rome-Berlin Axis Agreement. Italy and Germany pledged to support each other in the event of war.

Hitler planned to invade Poland next. He believed Polish people were inferior to Germans.

Mussolini (left) and Hitler had meetings in Germany to discuss their plans.

So, he thought Germany could conquer Poland quickly and easily.

The British and French decided the time for appeasement was over. They threatened Hitler with military action if he sent troops into Poland. Hitler believed this was an empty threat. And even if they did attack, Hitler didn't think their armies could stop him.

After World War I ended, the British government shrank its military to save money. In 1918, Britain's army had included 3.8 million soldiers. By 1922, it had just 230,000.

Meanwhile, Hitler had been building up his troops. The Treaty of Versailles limited the size of the German army to 100,000 soldiers. But by 1935, Hitler had an army of 550,000. And he planned to keep expanding.

Soviet leader Joseph Stalin was also concerned about Hitler's plans. Germany and the Soviet Union were enemies. If Germany invaded Poland, Hitler might attack the Soviet Union next. Stalin didn't think he could count on support from his former allies in Britain and France. So, he made a bold move. In August 1939, he made a deal with Hitler. They would work together to conquer Poland.

The huge German army swept quickly through Poland in September 1939.

On September 1, 1939, Germany invaded Poland. It used a massive force of 1.5 million soldiers. It also sent 2,000 planes and 2,500 tanks. Britain and France gave Hitler a choice. He could withdraw from Poland, or they would declare war. Hitler did not respond. So, on September 3, 1939, the two nations declared war on Germany. A second world war had begun.

B·36380

CHAPTER 7

THE WORLD AT WAR

At first, the fighting centered in Europe. Polish forces retreated as Germany invaded from the west. Two weeks later, Soviet soldiers marched into eastern Poland. Polish troops were stunned. The British and French could do little to help. By October 1939, Poland's government had fallen.

In September 1940, Germany, Italy, and Japan signed the Tripartite Pact. They wanted to show the world that they were united. They also hoped

German troops bombed and took over Poland's capital city, Warsaw.

to keep the United States from entering the war. They thought US leaders wouldn't want to fight all three countries at once.

Hitler was also planning another attack. The Germans and Soviets had worked together to attack Poland. But Hitler still saw the Soviets as enemies. He decided to break his agreement with Stalin. In June 1941, three million German troops entered the Soviet Union. This invasion was known as Operation Barbarossa. The German forces advanced quickly. But the Soviets put up a strong fight. After this attack, the Soviet Union joined the Allies.

Meanwhile, tensions between Japan and the United States were growing. In 1939, the US Navy's fleet moved from California to Pearl Harbor, Hawaii. US leaders hoped this move would discourage Japan from taking over more land.

Hitler's attack on the Soviet Union was brutal. German soldiers burned villages and killed thousands of people.

Japanese military leaders began to think a war with the United States could not be avoided. So, on December 7, 1941, they bombed the fleet at Pearl Harbor. They hoped to cause so much damage that the United States would give up and stay out of the war. Instead, the United States joined the fight on the side of the Allies. For the next four years, World War II would rage all around the world.

FOCUS ON

CAUSES OF WORLD WAR II

Write your answers on a separate piece of paper.

1. Write a paragraph describing the main ideas of Chapter 6.

2. Do you think the Allies could have prevented a second world war if they had responded differently to Germany? Why or why not?

3. In what country did Benito Mussolini rise to power?

A. Germany
B. Italy
C. France

4. What is one reason that many countries tried to avoid a war with Germany?

A. They were still recovering from World War I, which was very costly.
B. They were too powerful to care about what Hitler was doing.
C. They were too busy fighting in other wars with different countries.

Answer key on page 48.

GLOSSARY

appeasement
Giving people what they want in order to keep them calm or prevent conflict.

civilians
People who are not in the military.

Communism
A political system in which all property is owned by the government.

depression
A period of time when an area's economy struggles, prices rise, and people lose their jobs.

hyperinflation
An extreme increase in prices.

parliament
A group of people who make laws.

reparations
Payments to make up for war damage.

socialists
People supporting a political system in which the government provides for basic needs, and where workers control the economy.

strike
To stop working as a way to protest or call for change.

tactics
Planned actions that are used to achieve a certain goal.

treaty
An official agreement between groups or countries.

TO LEARN MORE

BOOKS

Fitzgerald, Stephanie. *Kristallnacht*. North Mankato, MN: Compass Point Books, 2018.

Mack-Jackson, Benjamin. *World War II History for Teens.* Emeryville, CA: Rockridge Press, 2021.

Taylor, Diane C. *World War II: From the Rise of the Nazi Party to the Dropping of the Atomic Bomb*. White River Junction, VT: Nomad Press, 2018.

NOTE TO EDUCATORS

Visit **www.focusreaders.com** to find lesson plans, activities, links, and other resources related to this title.

INDEX

Answer Key: 1. Answers will vary; **2.** Answers will vary; **3.** B; **4.** A